The God-Man Enigma

Dani Janes

The contemporary worldview of spirituality and religion desperately deserves theological and psychological fervor through revolutionaries such as Jung, Tillich, and Schleiermacher as the modern perspective creates an experience assumed to be had with God which lacks consciousness of such thinking and being. These men propose that modern rationality and scientific thought have since made great strides toward moving the human existence away from mindfulness of theological investments, and in turn prevent man from developing into his/her full humanity. This moves aspects of mankind's own divinity and the relationship between this chasm that divides divinity and humanity, as seen through the psychological lens. The aim then is finding the unique correlation between the psychic and spiritual components of man to best suit the comprehension of the self in rediscovery versus the unproductive nature of becoming too narrowly minded about anthropological existence that should not be centralized to only focus on the Christian audience but for all spiritually centered individuals, regardless of what faith tradition and practices one might adhere to, or the lack thereof. [1]Metaphysics is a resource for thinking about what it means to be a human being touched by God's revelation in Jesus Christ (Christ consciousness). This paper explores the intersection of theology and the psychology of Carl Jung. Specifically, I argue that Schleiermacher's understanding of Christology and Jung's notions of the conscious and unconscious mind, when put in conversation, result in an enhanced understanding of Christ consciousness.

Through such spiritual practices and study, specifically in Patanjali yoga, are seen the major focuses on metaphysics that deal in aspects of prakrti (spirit) and purusa (physical and psychic being) which find themselves closely related to that of Jung's theories of both the collective unconscious and the spirit (conscious) that are found to be a natural component of man which then leads into spiritual maturity through both empirical and mystical study of the psyche. I argue that along with Jung's approach, which delves into the direction of separation happening of opposition between the human mind and the cosmic reality, the yogic experience can be seen in duality through a waking consciousness and a deepening meditative existence that mirrors the unconscious mind. [2]

Paired with the psychological symbolism of the self in regard to the anima/animus of Jungian psychology, which can be seen as the unconscious, finds itself in dichotomy with the doctrine of sin and evil; re-imaged into the symbolism of Anti-Christ by Christian thought, and likewise debated as being what Jung would refer to as the shadow of the self that must be understood just as equally as the conscious mind in order to further have certain knowledge of the self and the Christian embodiment.[3] This is not to say that we should take extreme measures to find these states as being the low embodiment of consciousness, but I argue that we must come into clear understanding of ourselves from a masculine (animus) perspective that tends to rationalize and find gratitude in fulfilling desires, as well as the feminine (anima) that imbues the feminine aspects of the person through characteristics involving the Spirit and emotion, which are directly interconnected with the unconscious mind that can never truly be understood by the human prerogative, but rather embraced and learned from just as we see the depths of the infinite unknown, as we come to know these states of the unconscious mind.

Stepping into conversation to affirm with Jung, the ego (assumed personality i.e. the conscious mind) has the greatest difficulty with *self-knowledge* which deals directly with the unconscious mind. This bears the greatest importance as the conscious mind (ego) is separated from the self (unconscious) and remains in constant struggle with the ego as a means to find itself. This finds itself evident with example to the State mentality of government control over the minds and hearts of the public masses. No greater example of doctrine can be envisioned further than that of the indoctrinated church and the statutes that religion provide as truth. This is to say that the socio-political efforts have attempted to uproot the intention and efforts of the Church to further their agenda of power and restriction to belief and the mind. The ultimate result of this is no longer religion, but rather a creedal existence. This carries the greatest weight in reflection with the mind's independence oriented to an organized mind, who has accepted consciousness as something of a precondition that proves the psychic and spiritual nature existent. Thus, I propose the inquiry of internal reflection and meditation which must be made to see clearly where humanity is positioned in cosmic reality of time and place, as in relation with circumstance to society and belief and the rationality that finds itself invested in a spiritual tandem; as aligned with the intentions of Carl Gustav Jung. [4]

To formulate a proper reference of Carl Jung's work within the realm of psychology and theology alike, Jung's lingo and analogy must first be understood as it is seen throughout his master works relating to the subject of the psychology of the mind as it will be later discussed in lieu of *Christ consciousness*. Initially, Jung creates the abstract of the *ego* as being the subordinate portion of the mind that frame the innermost thoughts and desires that create a formulated groundwork for the foundation of the persona even beyond one's own *conscious* understanding of the self. Reaching further into the ether we can conceive *consciousness* as a state of affairs between the ego and the *unconscious* mind, which might be more commonly referred to as the sub-consciousmind that could be compared to an endless sea of possibilities. By its nature, consciousness is the supernatural intelligence of God which has no point of vantage, but is eternal and ever existing. My personal endorsement of Jung's work provided through study and practice maintains correspondence with belief; as my understanding of which to be coequal with religion and spirituality and equally an entity all within its own right.

And just like the light of man, so too exists darkness; Jung describes this darkness as the shadow of man that is a complex and dually a balance in the universe, as you cannot have the light without the darkness and good without evil as they complement one another, giving the fullest meaning to both entities, of which they would lack meaning otherwise. It would be important to note that the shadow still falls under the premise of the unconscious mind. There is also what Jung calls the *anima* and *animus*, in which the *anima* is acknowledged as the archetype of emotion, preying on the unconscious mind;anima being the female subconscious and the *animus* the male, all expressed through the active, masculine conscious mind. When the anima is paired up with the mental capacity of the male mind it serves to reflect on everything that is female so as to help the male understand his role in what he is; as an illustration of the consciousness of the mind and how it interacts with itself inside and outside of existence psychologically. The animus, from the Greek "Logos," gives the exact same formulated approach to the female mind as it reflects for her what it means to be masculine, so as to redirect her in what she needs to become from a feminine prerogative. I will predicate on the grounds of my own discernment that having a healthy understanding of one's own anima and animus is truthfully having a higher aspect of the one self, as Jung would agree. The *self*-archetype posits particular interest due to the nature of the self. As defined, the self is a culmination of all conscious reality with aspects of the unconscious that identify with the conscious, according to Jung. In other words, everything that mankind encounters in its lifetime, to include his/her dreams, all integrate into the personality that is acquired over the span of one's own existence; this is otherwise known as the self. [5]

In *Jung on Christianity*, Carl Gustav Jung makes great strides to incorporate a visible imagery of the Christ-likeness in man without distorting the claim of man assuming divinity in man, but rather projecting the aspect of the psycho-spiritual model that lays claim to the godhead as being understood through the soul of man, to be driven through the Holy Spirit. Several sources are then supporting this claim starting with the early church fathers. Origen states, "The imago Dei imprinted on the soul, not on the body, is an image of an image, for my soul is not directly the image of God, but is made after the likeness of the former image." This phrasing is crucial in concerning where mankind stands in relation to the divine, as in 'likeness' but not a direct reflection. This could offer only the concept of spiritual discernment to play a key role in making a reflection on or of a reflection from a spiritual and psychological stance. St. Augustine takes the matter a step further in his adaptation which reads, "The God-image is within, not in the body. Where understanding is, where the mind is, where the power of investigating truth is, there God has an image. But where man knows himself to be made after the image of God, there he knows there is something more in him than is given to the beasts." This brings us to our Christ image, where the manifested re-representation of God through man takes place, says Jung. Where I might propound to hypothesize on this in direct juxtaposition with Jung is dispensed through the allegory of Siddhartha Gautama, who is more commonly referred to as the Buddha.

If given the original Adam, before the fall, as a precursor of the Christ-likeness that all might achieve, then it can be understood that Christ like the second Adam, moves the individual away from sin and restores the believer in light of grace. St. Augustine said, "Therefore our end must be our perfection, but our perfection is Christ," which takes on greater meaning when our focus becomes on understanding the relationship between that God-image and one's own conception of that image. So, if humanity is a re-representation of an original, then humanity is united with it, as the mystical union of the chemical wedding takes place between the cosmic husband and wife; husband being Christ and his bride the soul of mankind as was the symbolism of the Middle Age Christian mystics. This reunification process is not only similarly understood with the reunification of Christ in the ascension, or even the baptism and transcendence moment, but can be directly related to our own relationship with the godhead; through the Son, whom is in the Father, all working through the Holy Spirit. This can be seen both from the psychological lens of coming into awareness through the conscious mind, or through the moment of conversion into faith as is my own recognition of both ideals through my own conception; which can and may also be seen as 'understanding.'

This process of restoration also takes on a psychological premise that can be seen as the process through the symbolic self, which takes into account the whole man, refers also to the collective unconscious that requires inspection of the mind as not totally approachable through the unconscious; but instead must work toward apocatastasis, the regeneration of an original state of being. Like the primordial Adam, or the Christ, one must seek to restore, not alter. What makes this of greater interest is that through the study of psychology, this wholesome character archetype is something that is stressed as something unknown until known. To restate this, the truest self isn't known until the individual is made conscious of themself, or through the process of illumination. Then can the individual begin to rework, through their integrity, discernment of the anamnesis that is taking place through Christ and God, and similarly through man and Christ. This is found nowhere more present outside of the New Testament than through the early Christian Gnostics who took a psychological approach to the matter of good and evil, influence in their teaching that Christ "cast off his *shadow* from himself." This is unmistakable from the shadow that Jung speaks of in his concepts of the self as my personal understanding will allow my mind to contrive and accept this into my own belief and psyche. If taken into account the instinctual self, Jung states that all maintain the animus of the animal, until which through understanding of these precepts is the seeker then brought out of that state of unconsciousness and edified into consciousness, or into the mind of Christ. For Jung, this brought about the notion that there was no other acceptable option but to find or seek enlightenment through revelation as the awakening of the self to be the dichotomy of the light and darkness parallel which hold tension with one another to play into the role of discernment of both mind and spirit.[6]

In *Christian Faith*, Schleiermacher outlines a vision of what is a portrayal of an overlay of possibilities where everything is interrelated as God consciousness. He states that this is especially true to matters of faith which revolves itself in matters of the whole existence of humanity and its relation to religious capacity. He openly discourses the diverse perception of consciousness as absolute wisdom and knowledge or fantastic delusion subjected to the human experience. One option, he presumes, would be that the individual would have an experience with God-consciousness that enables the person to have ability to evolve and increase in their humanity as beings of intellect and ethic, or instead being the result of human finitude, finding one separate and lacking which might promote the yielding of such improvement to inhibit the individual. We might associate this with Jung's concepts of the self and shadow, or ego and ego-death. Through my own careful adaptation of this preceding, the separateness that follows Schleiermacher's theology diminishes the inevitable and omnipotence that is God consciousness. Thus, if found to be resolute in determining without undermining the divine, whether it come from a religious or psychological perspective, proves to have definite logic and cohesion with humanity, as through my own perceptive study will allow my posture on the matter.

Taking the scientific approach, Schleiermacher also takes into account the notion of historical presence that might redirect personal bias in order to allow further insight on how matters of faith might have been proposed, had it not been for tradition. Now, suppose there lacked tradition or religious influence at all, then there would be speaking of historical statements which can only be backed up by matters of fact, as such is the case with science. If this scientific evolution were the elemental preclusion behind human origin and understanding, then it would serve as a valid and valuable instance to work forward from into discernment of God and consciousness altogether. Distinct from this, had humanity evolved from the notion of God-consciousness into the workings of faith, then it would still have presumably have had its conception that would involve the improvement of mankind from the earliest of beginnings, which would then support the previous statement; and is not at all outside of my own frame of reference regarding Schleiermacher.

Having prefaced the state of affairs regarding consciousness and divinity as God-consciousness brings us to the human experience. As consciousness is understood primarily to have precepts in language, more specifically speech and later writing, the mind begins to rationalize the movement away from animalistic behavior and primordial things, and into a more conscious reality that might be deemed divine; as it is uniquely higher in its existence within the whole of creation. Conceptualizing time in regard to scripture is something of a mystery as there has been very little evidence to promote certainty of when and how it all began, which raises a few important questions. First, if there is no logical sense of beginning, how then can it be rationalized within our own consciousness? Having this perception of a lack of perception is illustrated via Schleiermacher as to the relationship to mother and child, where without the influence and intellect of the maternal (or paternal) figure, the child is rendered to become self-conscious, with or without guidance is my proposal avowed.

This can also allude us to discover the child as being at a developmental state of consciousness as would be prescribed through the Holy Spirit as the child's spirit (or will) might influence their external environment around them internally from the earliest of beginnings. If we take the latter into consideration, then there is no mediator present, and yet there is all the same. We might allow ourselves the privilege of seeing the mediator as being the Spirit, and likewise as the conscious awareness of the human mind working in unison with the divine spark that can be seen evident. This also brings to question the state of Adam, the first human being. If there was a mediator present for instruction, then all the pieces fall into place and allow the story and timeline to continue, however if not then we are left questioning the development of the person. As human beings have tendency to be repetitive, so is the case in the process of learning through repetition and the association of familiarity that is then commit to memory.

Having this in mind as a point of interest provides the outlook that there needs to be an initial moment of influence, that might presumed to be God or even awareness that leads later into higher presuppositions of divinity. If we take into account even the earliest notions of man as being purely driven through instinct for survival and without any direction in existence other than intuitive assumption, there would be very little prospect to further the case as it would maintain itself to be beyond imagination. This is to say that, whether in direct relation with the God figure through the method of tradition that those in religious circles ascribe themselves to, or rather the inner intellect that is the inner God consciousness that promotes levels of awareness is all unanimously of the same essence, and remains advanced beyond refutation. Without the presence of consciousness, nothing would be within human capacity to achieve, and yet mankind is always achieving. [7] From my own existential point of view, this is entirely accurate as I live and breathe, so I am. Therefore, I fully defend Schleiermacher's theory of the historicity and presence that is presented as being outside of tradition, and yet likely to have had equal amount of influence on humanity.

Both Jung and Tillich make the modernity of the times relevant as they discuss humanity's move away from religion and the impact that it has and will have on the world to come in *Jung and Christianity in Dialogue,* through the means of progressive thought moving through society and the mainstream thought that has penetrated religious streams of consciousness. This might provoke those who know of both theologian and psychologist to take a closer look as this would include the religious and spiritual facets of understanding to relate directly with man's ability to experience both God as divinity and as consciousness. Coming from similar, yet differing backgrounds, Jung and Tillich believe that the idea and existence of God brings about the progressive nature in man to promote such ways of thinking that might look more rational than they normally would, taking credit for the work made possible through predecessors of the church and psychology alike. The issue at hand, both concur, is that there is the greatest loss in our humanity when simplifying religion to a substitution for ethics, or an additional supplementary element that redirects our character, rather than something most personal that is our very identity. In this said identity maintains the very link to the divine, which is in part the self which we has so eagerly been attempted to be reproduced and replaced with modernity in all sense of the word. I will espouse that this leads to not only spiritual poverty, but a lack of economy of what it means to be a human being and thus limiting the fullness of life altogether, as in accordance and conversation with both Jung and Tillich.

Taking matters to a higher degree, both Jung and Tillich agree that theology, specifically in the western tradition, have been responsible for the degeneration of religious tradition by proxy of moving the contemporary belief of the societal standard to the forefront beyond tradition, the humanities, and all governing bodies of the church. Where this hinders the modern believer is in gaining true clarity through the relationship between the individual and God to develop a depth and wealth of understanding of the ultimate intention behind religion to begin with. Where this becomes particularly interesting is that we have both well renowned psychologist and theologian meeting at a solid neutral position that can equally agree upon matters as they believe these truths to be evident; which might be seen symbolically through the eyes of the psychologist and revealed and transmitted divinely by way of the theologian interchangeably to a degree. In the highest reverence, this perspective only permits to support the efforts of the church rather than hinder it, amidst the initial apprehension that might be felt if reading this one might assume the worst, which is not the case that I advocate.

Such case in point shows Jung looking at the matter as being in direct relation to the unconscious mind, naturally; all while Tillich looks respectively at the prospect of logical understanding of spiritual religiosity as being a rationalization of the spiritual that he coins 'rational literalism.' Where both professionals truly work most cohesively happens to be when the ego is no longer given liberty to its own spiritual consciousness that would normally evaluate and make intelligible the symbolic nature of religion so far as to delve into the mind and expand its spiritual depths limitlessly. It is at this cross-section where man has deprived himself of all humanity, which investigates the unconscious mind to discover the spiritual rationality which appears to be the living reality of what depths and unknown possibilities life has to offer through the living Word, that is awareness of such life; which is also my own stance as a champion of such views of Tillich and Jung. My personal belief expands beyond belief, to be taken both figuratively and literally as a challenge toward the ever expansive congruence of consciousness into the ethereal cosmic consciousness, coming into fullness and unity.

 Bringing about the concept of symbolism, reverting back to the idea of the archetype of the self within the parameters of the self in Christ, Jung makes three supportive positions toward this level of Christological thinking, yet never labeled it as such. First, The God-Human Archetype, references the root essence of the making of humanity and the relational nature that is directed and interrelated to God. If taken into account the ego, then movement beyond the ego allows awareness to find the self, and beyond that to find the highest self which would then have divine aspects of infinitude that is the mind and soul; depending on which position taken theologically or psychologically. Once defined, the self can no longer have a true definition. That is, the self is not definitive if it remains infinite and full of possibility. At this plateau, might then be relinquished the mystery of the self as being ultimate reality. Jung would come to term this, 'cosmic correspondence,' that would tether the individual as the microcosmic entity and the world (cosmos) as the macrocosm. This is where the correspondence makes headway as the individual exists in both realities and yet remains individual to them both; to mean that the person finds themselves as an effective means to the greater good and also something finessed to have its own creative mark in time and space.

Where Jung takes us next relies solely on our aspect of God and the self. What reveals itself predominantly about his work is that the self is experienced as a process, or life itself which Jung also considers symbolic for God. This purports that through the inner workings of experiencing life, we find ourselves meeting the world and our truest nature simultaneously and thus manifesting the Imago Dei. Once discovering this imagery through symbolic and experienced existence gives the individual the necessary foundation to further move into their highest selves, which is within the context of the world to promote such unity and understanding to all. At the pinnacle of this would maintain that it would be absolute, but instead becomes other than. To assume to be absolute remains an absurdity according to Jung. Having such a severed and distanced relation with all provides no relationship or will to have any potential for God to maintain connected to man, thus this cannot be considered what belief asserts God to be. Having the intention and resource to make association through relatable interconnectedness makes sense of the God that Jung proclaims. And through the opposite end of the spectrum in relation to mankind, we find ourselves in introspective reflection to then discover ourselves through the process of self-realization, wherein found outside of the self what is beyond and also what is within; only to conclude that exists a moral and spiritual duty to work diligently with the raw ability is divinely given. Like Jung, I can contend that through the experience of existence, there divinity is experienced and known, which can be rationalized or worshiped, but still remains paramount in understanding as relational beings what and how divinity remains relatable.

Finally, when arriving at the Christ figure, it must be understood that the person of Jesus Christ was and is the full embodiment of the God-human archetype. To fathom such a complex condition, it must first be accepted that everyone has an archetype that can be compared to their ego or the collective of their existence which makes them who they consider themselves and ultimately, what leads them to become more of themselves than they ever knew to be initially. This would imply that through the archetype that Christ held, his uniqueness of having such a staple in history as being the ideal figure carried a weight with it as he found his true self to be wedged between the microcosmic and macrocosmic realities, which placed himself as prior being his potential self to then moving into the reality that was his actual self, the realized and ultimate existence of selfhood.

Having this perspective brings understanding of the omnipresent, omniscient, and omnipotent which now becomes other than, or rather more specifically experiencing himself in his own finitude as individual, as a sense of transcendence within that then expresses transcendence without. Factoring into account this transcendence comes in naming him "Son of God," as identified in his temporal identity as "Son of Man. This brings us back to, as Jung would aptly agree, to a state of homousia, as one in the same identity, of reality and essence. The unification of the two entities as one rather than anything other than requires that we first understand the self. [8]

Glimpsing at an abstract of the Trinitarian doctrine there is something of an ideal that Christianity has provided illustration for what precedes the process of the existential and metaphorical reality that is the trinity. If looking at the character of Christ as being the exemplary figure which should be modeled accordingly, it is then accepted that the Spirit is present as has been presented to Christ as then Christ delivered the Spirit to humanity. Now, from this point further there might have to imagine Christ as the catalyst behind the inner workings of the process of the trinity; although his physical reality was only a limited existence, the instruction left allows believers to further understand that the responsibility given to Christian believers is not only a matter of proclamation, but also something psychological in nature, in that the self becomes rationalized and the reality of the self presents itself as not only what is, but the process of this happening as being held captive by the Holy Spirit should be focused on primarily.

But this doesn't exactly answer the question behind the relation of the trinity to man, which I would like to further discuss. If it is believed that the Father imparted his breath, or life essence, into the Son, they then live on united. Secondly, if it is then accepted that through Christ presenting the Holy Spirit to believers, then it must determine that the Spirit breaths with those who believe also. Now, if this is so, those who follow these indoctrinated pools of thought are encapsulated wholly, as believers in Christ share the same likeness and are aspects of one another. Just as Christ said 'Ye are gods' (John 10:34) sheds light on this matter directly, and leaves very little room for exploration being as direct and clear as could possibly be. Jung seems to have an issue with the natural theology that takes place in the trinity involving the terminology of Father, Son, and Holy Spirit; as he might understand this to also have the option or possibility of being Father, Son, and Mother, if we take into account the natural order; and why not? Well, aside from natural order, it must take into account the phenomenon of the psyche and how this might weave a web of discord within the psychology of humanity, as to understand the functioning behind why this might have taken place. Not to prove whether this being a matter of ethics, but rather to understand the purpose behind the institution taking hold of the doctrine.

When taken into account matters of the essence of God-breathed life and also the soul of all living creatures, especially within the context of the Holy Spirit, there can be seen a stark contrast between the two accordingly. In the belief of the Egyptian ancients, Father and son are in hypostatic union as one in the same soul known as 'Ka-mutef' and are incidentally no different than the Christian counterpart wherein God-breathed life of the Spirit throughout the Trinitarian understanding of God. One issue that comes from the view of the Trinitarian doctrine might affect the psychological perspective that man has had regarding the placement of itself within the equation of the Spirit's inner workings of the hypostasis as being illogical at best, due to the intention colliding with the ill represented divinity and man as having too relatable a likeness, to be misrepresented as the same. The early Gnostics attempted to reveal the answer as interpreting and representing the Spirit as the mother picture, however this too had repercussion as it disembodied the paternal imagery as something other than, which hasn't been entirely excluded by the church, but is not the overarching theme of doctrine. This might also suppose that there is divine lineage between the godhead and man, which would disturb the order of worship and interpretation. To have a proper reverberation of the logic behind the Trinitarian doctrine, it is most important that we bring to light the enigma that is the mystery behind the Spirit, which is enclosed within itself.

Dualities have the privilege of presenting the paradox of their relational meaning as being a third entity outside of themselves and thus, having a third aspect that is esoteric and existential dually, provides the perfect dichotomy which also prevents polytheism as we see the division and unification between the One and other. Coming from a more metaphysical approach, through all of humanity's achievements, the levels of cognitive effort are the broadening of the collective unconscious which develops the overall consciousness. In turn, this cannot be completely understood as having complete independence, as this intelligence is irreprehensibly divine as the God-mind is the archetype that promotes this act of life that God manifests himself through. The trinity, seen and not understood due to its full complexity, remains symbolic in nature of both divinity and humanity as one entity, and yet other than. It is my firm conviction that humanity serves to be in this same ruling as 'other than,' as we are not truly divine nor are we entirely creatures of nature, being that we exist as physical beings and yet have intellect that precedes as the soul, that we then interpret as spirit being shepherded by the divine Spirit, in my own correspondence with Jung's interpretation of this psycho-spiritual model.

When man assumes to be entirely conscious of himself, the world around him, and outside of conventional ways of thinking, he has now assumed the ultimate assumption that is the ego. When man has become so self-involved then limitations have been constructed which hinder man. Thus, mankind separates itself from the unconscious, and thus the conscious, to become predominantly a perverted introversion of the true self that becomes more reactive than proactive in nature and thought. When thinking of the divine, there needs be an allowance of understanding to wander temporarily as such immaculate concepts remain beyond ability of the human mind to comprehend. God, through the understanding of man, holds the greatest weight in the unconscious mind where most revelation is provided and personified. This allows such metaphysical concepts to build relationally within the human mind and soul. [9]

Kevin W. Hector writes in his article *Actualism and Incarnation: The High Christology of Friedrich Schleiermacher*, what he believes to be an account of the high theology of Schleiermacher's Christology as academically fulfilled and accurately driven. Through Hector's analysis, Schleiermacher looks at Christ as having a dualism, which carries the likeness of docetism, and yet his belief is what he calls 'actualism.' This mode of interpretation leads into terms of the relational aspect of Christology as seen through the act that is presented or carried out. This also presumes Christ's nature as being incarnate, however unique to western understanding of incarnation. This would entail the entirety of God's being which is represented throughout every moment that was Christ's life as the act that made Christ not like God, but God, incarnate as living this reality out. Reiterating the docetic account of Schleiermacher, it is often understood to have the dualism of Christ denying the fullness of divinity and also as having a compromised humanity. The individual might find them self caught in this paradox when ascending into higher states of awareness, as could be on account via Schleiermacher, and of my own accord through a higher understanding that the mind might serve in likeness of Christ by means of achievement of this 'Christ-like' mindedness that all are capable of.

If read from the angle of the archetype into what Schleiermacher calls 'archetypal humanity' it is then provided with a widened sense of clarity outside of the more rationalized doctrine of the incarnational person of Christ. Once the bonds of dogmatic indoctrination are broken, then it can be seen in accordance with Schleiermacher, although a renowned theologian, his views here lean toward the psychological and even the metaphysical as he revisits Christ as righteous in his humanity, and furthermore the most high of all human beings. This reveals an extraordinary account outside of what the traditional western perception might deem to allow as acceptable, and yet it proves to be eerily rational in his thoughtfulness.

To further the account, Schleiermacher understood the terms and conditions of his Christology as being repugnant to most theologies and doctrines, as he then proceeded to clarify that although Christ held the highest divinity among all of humanity, this exaltation is merely a matter of a degree; an act of measurement or level of education and understanding, even consciousness when thought of psychologically. Many take Schleiermacher's theology to be low in terms of its inability to describe the complex levels of divinity that is Christ, instead of the more literalistic and rationalized view of humanity that he alludes to. However, it is interesting to see that concurrently there exists an attack on the humanity of Schleiermacher's introspective on Christ as being less than fully human, that is Docetism at its finest, according to the masses. Having such grounds to speak on Christ promotes a figure that takes the latter route of the intercessory path that treads lines of tradition and contemporary theologies. This speaks to both parties when Christ is seen now as other than, both entities but also other than human and divine, which affiliates to no party particularly whether taken the philosophical aspects of humanity, or the theological of divinity, but now the figure has become transformed into the truly supernatural as not a phantasm but the quintessential utopian representative of both realities that we might coin Schleiermacher's actualism.

What Schleiermacher provides that is key toward recognition is that while this account happened as a matter of human history, it extends out of human reach, which also comes to dependence on a resource other than our own, i.e. God. This active method of thinking forwards conceptions of the incarnation as an active existence that is divinity. If we find ourselves completely dependent upon God, then the divine has absolute influence on our lives, without the subjection of humanity influencing God. However, if deity was dependent upon humanity, even slightly, then it would void our dependence upon God, says Schleiermacher. With this level of discernment, it can be concluded that God and the incarnation united are an active, not passive, existence dependent completely upon itself. Thus, even the finitude of the temporal selfhood of the man that was Christ could not be subject to the dependence man has relationally with God, making Christ an entity outside of, or other than, as he is the acting principle just as God is, dependent upon himself and God as one. Where this distinction plays into the human counterpart is in context on the basis of love that is this activity. Through the act of love we find the unification of both humanity and divinity, which is seen in the account of Christ as the love of God as God himself is this act of love. This supports the argument of God's love as being the action of Christ's motive which is then the incarnation, not an ideal, but an existing counterpart that is the act of God now the act also of Christ. [10]

Jung, in this study titled *Quantum Physics and the Spiritual Mind: A Mystical Vision of the Twenty-First Century* written by Lothar Shafer and Diogo Ponte, outlines a significant correlation between science and the supernatural aspects of that are quantum physics and the psychology of the spiritual element present in humanity. Discussing the aspects of how the world is perceived, Rene' Descartes allowed Western culture to the dualism of the materialism that runs most of the corporate world, and second the spiritual that deals solely with the minds of men and women. This had a severe effect on the universal thinking globally as Darwin soon after proposed his theory of evolution which then brought about much conflict within the realms of religion and spirituality, ethics, philosophy and the humanities. Jung made his formal statement which stated that the universal mind is driven through the structural archetypes, which have no physical mass or material form, exist as a psychic component that remains alien to nature and yet it exists all the same. This would have a drastic implication within the sciences, particularly quantum physics as it was now directed at proving that the materialistic existence was, in fact, non-materialistic in nature, as is the psychic mind. Thus, when information is carried out, it is being emanated from an outer source of the material existence and then materialized, exactly as thought is materialized. This breakthrough allowed the world to gain a new found perspective on itself that it might not have known prior to such discovery as we then allowing the self to have a quantitative and informed foundation for the interconnected unity of all consciousness throughout the cosmos.

Having a firm understanding in quantum physics allows one to conceive the facts just as they are, that what exists in the assessment of reality and the physical world is quite the opposite which is non-material, if we follow Schrodinger's quantum mechanics; this study remains the only existing theory that states the fundamental existence of atoms and molecules as having electrons which are not composed of matter but of energy waves. Likewise the mass of the atom is contained within the nucleus which is mostly charged energy, not physical mass, and yet the electrons contain mass and yet remain standing waves. Thus, to review, reality is not solely material as we most often assume it to be, and yet is a complete phenomenon of the senses as being something other than; when instead the reality transcends this materialism that we are given to believe is the ultimate reality of non-materialism. [11]

In Hildegard, Jung, and the Dark Side of God Clendenen uncovers a matter most theologians and religiously minded individuals have difficulty treading around, and that is the matter of theodicy, as presented through the minds of the twelfth century Benedictine theologian and saint Hildegard von Bingen, and twentieth century Swiss psychologist and psychoanalyst, Carl Gustav Jung. Theodicy, having the controversial nature of an all supreme deity which has all control and order of creation and humanity then becomes scrutinized and put under fire of questioning by the rationality of logic that inquires the natural state of things and why such negative outcomes arise within and without history. Jung had a difficult time ascribing to an absolute power that he could not connect and relate to, as the traditional methods of religion he had been brought up with had taught. Instead, his whole rationality was revolving around the unconscious mind due to the nature of the church's implement of his era to hold the mind of the believer captive in childlike mindedness spiritually and religiously as they grew into adulthood and into an awakened consciousness. Hildegard held a similar sentiment in her waking consciousness as Pope Asastasias IV compelled her to follow her discernment, which would sit with her throughout the remainder of her life and ministry and would be repeated through the words of Jung some eight hundred years later.

Both Hildegard and Jung were concerned that the modern western thought and practice of Christianity had such a one-sided and narrowed vision of spirituality that it lessened the transformative nature of the spirit through the process of change that should properly occur within the individual and the intellect of the individual as promoted through the symbolism, traditions, and practices; which, to Jung, had transformed into something he called "obscure anachronisms" that had failed to advance the mental and spiritual maturity of the soul, and instead found itself holding the mind and soul hostage to its precepts. The transformation, according to both Hildegard and Jung, might best be summarized as to the work of the *Dark Night of the Soul*, where the believer ventures into the treacherous unknown, through suffering of heart, be it the endurance that is the product of this suffering at some point when we come in contact with our shadow or the darkness of God, the unconscious, or the unknown. When moved from states of difficulty that promote rigidity in the life of faith, can then be experienced the completeness of our character providing hope as this opens new vistas into the limitless beyond confusion and unintelligible understandings. Both theologian and psychologist found this dark night or confrontation with their most daunting aspects of themselves and where their faith stood as the moments of clarity which allowed them the genius that they held. [12]

In G. Clarke Chapman's study of *Jung and Christology* there is an immediate reference toward Jung's psychology of Christ as to have symbolized Jesus as a prestigious and highly educated rabbi who found himself in the archetype of the self as he discovered the underlying concept of the tradition that he was raised to believe and know, and likewise having found the archetypal self, he was understood to have shed the shadow of the self. This should have implication for every follower of Christ as to have sacrificed themselves in order to gain the kingdom, not on a literal plane, but metaphysical. Not only because Christ himself had carried out the ultimate representation by fulfilling the motif on all planes of logic, whether it be intentional or not, the result became the highest pinnacle of humanity as his existence and death were and still are the apex of our capability in understanding and humility.

Although coming from a very sectarian view of Christianity, Jung considered himself Christian, with the implication that there was a depth of psychological prose that hadn't been yet unveiled since the time of the Council of Chalcedon (451 AD) which had negated to make the dichotomy of the divinity and humanity of Christ as relevant to humanity, and intelligible enough for lay people and the educated to ingest in context to make sensible the truths that it deems necessary for life and spirituality to take place. As human beings expand their consciousness, so too do they realize that they themselves are teleological in nature, that is curious for understanding, or yearning for what hasn't made itself available to the conscious awareness from the unconscious mind.

Christ became something definitively symbolic and other worldly, even beyond the guidelines of both psychology and religion as it occurred to him as spiritual, and even metaphysical; which brings about the mystical aspect behind the unknown unconscious mind. What Jung believed is that Christ had been blessed with a level of intelligence of a certain gifted acumen toward the most ancient of all archeological discoveries, which refers directly to the collective unconscious mind and how the archetypes of the mind directed the course of human history to every relative point in time, and likewise at his moment in time being that he was uniquely a historical landmark in humanity and also the metaphysical metaphor of the archetype of perfected humanity. You might look at the figure of Christ through this light as an entrepreneur among a massive order of failed attempts to build a sustainable and sensible existence that most all individuals can circumscribe themselves with. Having such language as 'Son of Man' resourced through the book of Enoch, there became an allusion of an awakened sense of self among the local Galilean population of Christ's time to pursue greater avenues of thought and to penetrate the mind in such a way that we might know the self to know God and also to know God that we might know ourselves.

This heightened sense of symbology also speaks to the reincarnation of the Easter event. Jung believed that rather than ascribing a literal interpretation of living a life that shadows and attempts to mimic Christ, we should accept ourselves from where we stand as Christ himself accepted his own uniqueness and so found divinity in his archetypal self. Thus, the phraseology, "Imitation of Christ," might be viewed as living lives of the highest sincerity and seeking truth lifelong until illumination delivers us to these truths that make us ultimately unique, and then can our humanity find itself situated in line with divinity. This does not mean to debunk or dismiss traditional views or beliefs in the Christian message, but rather to enlighten the reader to an outside perspective that might challenge and inspire that would progress faith, and not diminish it. Quoting Jung, "The essence of Christian tradition is by no means the simple man Jesus whom we seek in vain in the Gospels, but the lore of the God-man and his cosmic drama." This moves the conversation into a more deliberate understanding of the collective unconscious and the man that made this vision visible.[13]

As interpreted through the eyes of Allegra de Laurentiis in *Hegel and Metaphysics: On Logic and Ontology in The System* indicates that running rampant amidst the world lies the hindrance of metaphysical thought with such giants as Kant, Heidegger and Popper, to name a few. With these individuals come the influence they carry with the likes of radical empiricism, and pragmatism as the basis of rational thought. The scientific method is a relatively new age concept in the grand scheme of development of ideals and moving hypotheses into theory, and theory into matters of fact; these concepts that assert truth, are only half truths as they can only prove what can be understood through the primal senses, which also provides the necessary leverage for logic, which is also a construct in of itself that man takes precedence over without paying dues to the divine consciousness that pervades all of the cosmic order.

Hegel believed that metaphysics implied the science or study of the object of reason; Aristotle believed a similar notion in that he claimed it was the first causes and principles of being, or the absolute reality: the soul, universe, and God. First, from the objective was created the phantasm of the phenomenal that is the soul. Second, the universe is believed to be the complete objectivity in its wholeness. And third, God is the absolute reality in that connects and overshadows and engulfs all through both thought and being. To quote Hegel "Truth, in that supreme sense in which God and God only is the Truth," brings the sincerest light to this sentiment. This level of thinking transcends the natural order of contemporary theologies as it ascertains and defends itself in its wisdom. Where faith maintains an absolute certainty through intuition, metaphysics redirects that faith in a manner that provides introspective and reflective thinking that is systematized to broaden the understanding of the believer and non-believer alike through truth which both parties can agree upon. [14]

Edwards makes strides unparalleled when discussing the transcript from *Jesus and the Cosmos*, where he draws his inspirational wisdom from the late Karl Rahner who made an attempt at exacting the comparative nature between evolution and Christology, as we come to understand the incarnation as it parallels modern science. Edwards developed a systematic approach through three principles that paved a way for process theologians to gain momentum to trek the unexplored territory. First, Rahner exposits Jesus as a "self-transcendence of the cosmos toward God." We need to carefully and thoughtfully uncover this as to not miss what his intention was. The self-transcendence of the cosmos should not be taken lightly, as it would posit the self of man in the highest degree of all creation, time, and space moving directionally toward a divine ideal. If this concept is received as merely divine then one might take it as it was initially delivered, to assume primarily the sole relation between Christ and God, however, if we take into account the humanity that was apparent in the person of the man that was Jesus; we might also find that this is a continual process that was always evolving within Jesus, as it is with all of humanity and all creation. Edward's second point likens to the inner-relationship that is implicitly driven through the communication of God with mankind through His grace which manifests itself in the action of the living Logos that became Jesus of Nazareth. And thirdly, and most profoundly, the reverberation of God can be understood from the vantage of God's own perspective as His own communicative process with the cosmos. Edwards describes this matrix as such "In God's self-bestowal in Jesus of Nazareth, first, God accepts the cosmos definitively and irrevocably. And second, the cosmos accepts God definitively and irrevocably, and third, these two acceptances are manifested in our history as constituting a real unity in the one Jesus of Nazareth."

Rahner also comments on his work *Foundations of Christian Faith* to explore further a more scientifically rationalized conceptualization of Christology as interpreted from the discipline of evolutionary theology, respectively of both the figure of Christ and the worldview that became of the momentum that grew from the person and hypostatic union of His humanity and divinity. Having a perspective of contemporary incarnation, one might awe at the intrinsic happening that is the grace that all creatures high and low are given such heights of this hypostatic union with Christ as the self-sacrificing God in all of us, as God in self-communicative mindfulness. As another outside resource, John Cobb Jr. coming from a background of process theology imparts what he knows as "Transcendent Logos," as an immanence that occurs in all things through the initial order in creative purpose; or actualizing (gaining consciousness of) itself; but nowhere as drastically can this be interpreted than it has been through the course of humanity. Cobb views "Christ" as the transformative evolution of the transcendence within and without the world, where humanity sits at the apex of all existence. [15]

Paul Tillich provides a much needed sigh of relief in his approach to God through concepts that run alongside contentions such as estrangement and the unification from estrangement. He pulls these adaptations from his essay *The Two Types of Philosophy of Religion* where he makes efforts to harmonize the mind of modernity and contemporary ideals of religion. Both theologian and philosopher find themselves in the context of such thinking, says Tillich that through necessary studious persistence they attain knowledge to build upon wisdom through certain levels of awareness; or as Jung might relate, consciousness. As Tillich would consider the divine, he states, "I approach God as one 'unknown' who happens to come in my orbit. I make statements about him in terms of doubt and possibility and perhaps probability. I am at first suspicious, then friendly towards him, and may even become his friend. And he, as the more powerful and more perfect one, may give me support, direction and mercy; he may reveal himself to me within the limits of our remaining alienation. But all this is accidental for both of us."

What a curious and thought provoking statement Tillich provides us with to grapple. It screams of conviction for and against the contention of theism, and yet in its irony finds estrangement in the lack of relationship with God, as the personification here is lacking, and thus the self is not made visible, but instead other than. This will prove to be a valuable opening as both the dogma and critical methods given through such theologies of theologians like Barth are contended with vigor and passion. With a more obscure approach, Tillich sees God as a fleeting existence, just as the concept of life and moments that are fleeting. With this method of thought, we may not ever discover the utmost certainty about God or the self, but the limitless in probability of the unknown and unattainable that the divine is said to be. Standing amidst the definitive, or rather the doctrinal and dogmatic might accelerate the learning curve relationally toward divine understanding as this method surely gives more possibility in reference to overcoming estrangement from God, and the self. Having the uniqueness is uniquely human, and in sensitivity allows the floodgates to open the truth of the character of both God and man and God within man as reflective of the self.

Tillich takes on the most abstract inspiration through his ideals and philosophies of being as his ground is rooted in the richness of symbolism that he believes is where the process of being takes formation. Contrasting the Buddhist interpretation of being as working toward the object of nothingness as the holy other, there is a shape that is forming itself through the ascending transition into transcendence, which being eternal, overcomes form through immanence. Unlike the influence of Calvinism, cosmology defines itself through certainty of perceptions of intuitive reasoning. Through this process of coming into awareness, empirical thought that focuses on data and what can be mustered through the providential according to modern rationalization and logic; rather this is a matter of metaphysical thought that considers the plausibility of the unknown that holds equal amount of authority among the religious and spiritual communities, philosophers, theologians, educators and the like.

Tillich's chasm between faith and belief come to light in his *Systematic Theology* as he delivers the controversy of the formal and the material as being the traditional and solidified doctrinal belief of Christianity, as where his own dissemination gathers his subjective prerogative moving from one essence to another. This would suggest absolute being, or rather existence; as faith in the act of being and having a life worth meaning. Tillich also references his hypothesis on the meaning behind what he considers absolute faith. This would find itself evident again simply in the act of being, having defeated the angst and fear of non-being through doubt and loss of self. Tillich said, there are no regulative legalities with absolute faith like there are present in doctrine however there is substance and rhetoric. In order for faith to become absolute Tillich has three precepts that must be met: First, he states that the experience of power of being itself manifests in life, which at all costs defends itself against despair and the judgment of the self and wavering uncertainty. Second, dependence upon non-being through experience of absolute being. And third, to accept acceptance; that is, of being accepted. [16]

Moving forward into eternity, we now have a certain aspect of reality that might not have found itself manifest prior to this study, which was the hope and inspiration worth reflection. Having firm foundation in the logic of the self and the ego can help guide us into the most ultimate dimensions of reality that we might consider consciousness, and others might refer to as God. Christ, in His selfless and hopeful ideal, promoted such teaching to have a meditative and thoughtful perspective on life to know ourselves fully that we too may know God as He came to know God and the self, Himself. Denial of such divisions of the persona and the self, such as the ego and the shadow is futile to understanding creation as it has an ebb and flow, that it must contain both the darkness with the light so that there might be order made of chaos, due to its very nature, there cannot be chaos without order and without order chaos has no depth. Thus, we struggle to understand ourselves and

God through due process, but without the struggle progress cannot exist.

Having faith is a matter of faith, just like existence is exactly what it purports itself to be, in its very existence so too it is. This is the matter of being, simply to be, with the condition that this existence is ever transcending into greater heights of understanding. Having the vantage of pursuing the unknown, unconscious mind that is the mind of God precludes nothing, but instead allows the mind to reach into the furthest recesses which is where we come to know God. There can be found meaning in life out of the abstract, symbolic spark that appears as something out of nothing is the mind of God. This is the calling that we find knocking at our front door at all hours of the night, begging our attention and passion. We all contain the immanence of the hypostatic union if we choose to look beyond the veil and ascribe ourselves to the love and thought provoking limitlessness of our sub-conscious when we become totally aware. Finding awareness begins through the process of accepting ourselves exactly where we are, not to amount to nothing and find ourselves surrounded in void as Buddhism promotes, but to find the unanimity of voice that is the absolute intelligence that teaches fervor and grace, where we too find peace in knowing. Thinking about God reveals that we think of God, and as such, in provoking the Spirit to assist us in becoming more ourselves as we walk figuratively, and live not metaphorically but literally. Life then becomes all the more meaningful once thought about as a wholesome concept that remains eternal, such as God and consciousness.

Bibliography

Moore, Robert L., and Daniel J. Meckel. 1990. *Jung and Christianity in Dialogue: Faith, Feminism, and Hermeneutic.* Jung and Spirituality Series. New York: Paulist Press, c1990. https://apts.idm.oclc.org/login?url=https://search.ebscohost.com/login.aspx?direct=true&db=cat03946a&AN=APTS.36449&site=eds-live&scope=site.

Coward, Harold G. 1985. *Jung and Eastern Thought.* SUNY Series in Transpersonal and Humanistic Psychology. Albany, N.Y.: State University of New York Press, c1985. https://apts.idm.oclc.org/login?url=https://search.ebscohost.com/login.aspx?direct=true&db=cat03946a&AN=APTS.29209&site=eds-live&scope=site.

Jung, C. G., and Murray Stein. 1999. *Jung on Christianity.* Princeton Paperbacks. Princeton, N.J.: Princeton University Press, c1999. https://apts.idm.oclc.org/login?url=https://search.ebscohost.com/login.aspx?direct=true&db=cat03946a&AN=APTS.289362&site=eds-live&scope=site.

Jung, C. G. 1958. *The Undiscovered Self.* Boston, Little, Brown [1958].

https://apts.idm.oclc.org/login?url=https://search.ebscoh
ost.com/login.aspx?direct=true&db=cat03946a&AN=APTS.
1326&site=eds-live&scope=site.

Jung, C. G. 1978. *Aion□: Researches into the Phenomenology of
the Self*. Bollingen Series: 20. Princeton University Press.
https://apts.idm.oclc.org/login?url=https://search.ebscoh
ost.com/login.aspx?direct=true&db=cat03946a&AN=APTS.
260486&site=eds-live&scope=site.

Jung, C. G., and Murray Stein. 2012. *Jung on Christianity*.
Princeton: Princeton University Press.
https://apts.idm.oclc.org/login?url=https://search.ebscoh
ost.com/login.aspx?direct=true&db=nlebk&AN=435361&sit
e=eds-live&scope=site.

Schleiermacher, Friedrich, Terrence N. Tice, Catherine L.
Kelsey, and Edwina G. Lawler. 2016. *Christian Faith□: A New
Translation and Critical Edition*. Westminster John Knox
Press.
https://apts.idm.oclc.org/login?url=https://search.ebscoh
ost.com/login.aspx?direct=true&db=cat03946a&AN=APTS.
302450&site=eds-live&scope=site.

Moore, Robert L., and Daniel J. Meckel. 1990. *Jung and
Christianity in Dialogue□: Faith, Feminism, and Hermeneutic*.
Jung and Spirituality Series. New York□: Paulist Press,
c1990.
https://apts.idm.oclc.org/login?url=https://search.ebscoh
ost.com/login.aspx?direct=true&db=cat03946a&AN=APTS.
36449&site=eds-live&scope=site.

Jung, C. G., Herbert Edward Read Sir, Michael Fordham,
and Gerhard Adler. 1953. *The Collected Works of C. G. Jung*.
Bollingen Series: 20. Pantheon Books.
https://apts.idm.oclc.org/login?url=https://search.ebscoh
ost.com/login.aspx?direct=true&db=cat03946a&AN=APTS.
13716&site=eds-live&scope=site.

Hector, Kevin W. 2006. "Actualism and Incarnation: The
High Christology of Friedrich Schleiermacher." *International*

Journal of Systematic Theology 8 (3): 307–22. doi:10.1111/j.1468-2400.2006.00216.x.

Lothar Schäfer, and Diogo Valadas Ponte. 2013. "Carl Gustav Jung, Quantum Physics and the Spiritual Mind: A Mystical Vision of the Twenty-First Century." *Behavioral Sciences*, no. 4: 601. doi:10.3390/bs3040601.

Clendenen, Avis. 2010. "Hildegard, Jung, and the Dark Side of God." *Magistra* 16 (2): 26–76. https://search.ebscohost.com/login.aspx?direct=true&db=a9h&AN=57276666&site=ehost-live&scope=site.

Chapman, G Clarke, Jr. 1997. "Jung and Christology." *Journal of Psychology & Theology* 25 (4): 414–26. https://search.ebscohost.com/login.aspx?direct=true&db=lsdah&AN=ATLA0001019920&site=ehost-live&scope=site.

Laurentiis, Allegra de. 2016. *Hegel and Metaphysics⬚: On Logic and Ontology in the System.* Hegel-Jahrbuch / Sonderband. [N.p.]: De Gruyter. https://search.ebscohost.com/login.aspx?direct=true&db=nlebk&AN=1221910&site=ehost-live&scope=site.

Shults, F. LeRon. 2008. *Christology and Science.* Ashgate Science and Religion Series. Grand Rapids, Mich. https://search.ebscohost.com/login.aspx?direct=true&db=cat03946a&AN=APTS.142121&site=ehost-live&scope=site.

Re Manning, Russell, and Samuel Shearn. 2018. *Returning to Tillich⬚: Theology and Legacy in Transition.* Tillich Research = Tillich-Forschungen = Recherches Sur Tillich. Berlin: De Gruyter. https://search.ebscohost.com/login.aspx?direct=true&db=e000xna&AN=1658992&site=ehost-live&scope=site.

Notes

[←1]

Moore, Robert L., and Daniel J. Meckel. 1990. *Jung and Christianity in Dialogue : Faith, Feminism, and Hermeneutic.* Jung and Spirituality Series. New York : Paulist Press, c1990.
https://apts.idm.oclc.org/login?url=https://search.ebscohost.com/login.aspx?direct=true&db=cat03946a&AN=APTS.36449&site=eds-live&scope=site.

[←2]

Coward, Harold G. 1985. *Jung and Eastern Thought*. SUNY Series in Transpersonal and Humanistic Psychology. Albany, N.Y.□: State University of New York Press, c1985.
https://apts.idm.oclc.org/login?url=https://search.ebscohost.com/login.aspx?direct=true&db=cat03946a&AN=APTS.29209&site=eds-live&scope=site.

    *See also Johnson, Charles *The Yoga Sutras of Patanjali: The Book of The Spiritual Man*; specifically books I and II. These works target the regenerative aspects of spiritual rebirth via the psyche, as made an example by the Apostle Paul while in Corinth. Johnson retorts that the psychical man is in essence spiritual, and that the psyche becomes the unveiling of prophecy.

[←3]

Jung, C. G., and Murray Stein. 1999. *Jung on Christianity.* Princeton Paperbacks. Princeton, N.J.□: Princeton University Press, c1999.
https://apts.idm.oclc.org/login?url=https://search.ebscohost.com/login.aspx?direct=true&db=cat03946a&AN=APTS.289362&site=eds-live&scope=site.

[←4]

Jung, C. G. 1958. *The Undiscovered Self.* Boston, Little, Brown [1958]. https://apts.idm.oclc.org/login?url=https://search.ebscohost.com/login.aspx?direct=true&db=cat03946a&AN=APTS.1326&site=eds-live&scope=site.

*See *Collected Works of C.G. Jung, Vol. 9* (Part 2) which addresses the shadow as a moral problem wherein the dark aspects of the persona meet with self-knowledge to trace inferior traits to reveal unnecessary: emotional instabilities, autonomous behaviors, obsessive and possessive natures etc.

[←5]

Jung, C. G. 1978. *Aion : Researches into the Phenomenology of the Self.* Bollingen Series: 20. Princeton University Press. https://apts.idm.oclc.org/login?url=https://search.ebscohost.com/login.aspx?direct=true&db=cat03946a&AN=APTS.260486&site=eds-live&scope=site.

[←6]

Jung, C. G., and Murray Stein. 2012. *Jung on Christianity.* Princeton: Princeton University Press. https://apts.idm.oclc.org/login?url=https://search.ebscohost.com/login.aspx?direct=true&db=nlebk&AN=435361&site=eds-live&scope=site.

*See Dynner, Glenn's Title: Holy Dissent: Jewish and Christian Mystics in Eastern Europe. This study provides the mystical symbology through kabbalistic motif as a service to promote the truths of Christianity through psyche and spirituality as evident. These hermeneutics are drawn from early Jewish esoteric thought that are disclosed to all, but founded in truth and modesty. Spec. found in Book II, Chapter I.

[←7]

Schleiermacher, Friedrich, Terrence N. Tice, Catherine L. Kelsey, and Edwina G. Lawler. 2016. *Christian Faith□: A New Translation and Critical Edition*. Westminster John Knox Press. https://apts.idm.oclc.org/login?url=https://search.ebscohost.com/login.aspx?direct=true&db=cat03946a&AN=APTS.302450&site=eds-live&scope=site.

[←8]

Moore, Robert L., and Daniel J. Meckel. 1990. *Jung and Christianity in Dialogue□: Faith, Feminism, and Hermeneutic.* Jung and Spirituality Series. New York□: Paulist Press, c1990. https://apts.idm.oclc.org/login?url=https://search.ebscohost.com/login.aspx?direct=true&db=cat03946a&AN=APTS.36449&site=eds-live&scope=site.

*See Dourley, John P. *C.G. Jung and Paul Tillich : The Psyche As Sacrament*, Ch. 2 'The Psyche as Sacrament,' which highlights the exploration of the depths of man's psyche that moves beyond rational thought and into something ethereal that can only be exposited by the symbol alone. When this is taken into account, both Tillich and Jung give adequate response to the loss of self through contemporary thoughts of rationality wherein the symbolic self and spiritual are being lost; thus they contend to bring about a greater rigor for understanding the overview of spirituality through course of religion and reason.

[←9]

Jung, C. G., Herbert Edward Read Sir, Michael Fordham, and Gerhard Adler. 1953. *The Collected Works of C. G. Jung*. Bollingen Series: 20. Pantheon Books. https://apts.idm.oclc.org/login?url=https://search.ebscohost.com/login.aspx?direct=true&db=cat03946a&AN=APTS.13716&site=eds-live&scope=site.

[←10]

Hector, Kevin W. 2006. "Actualism and Incarnation: The High Christology of Friedrich Schleiermacher." *International Journal of Systematic Theology* 8 (3): 307–22. doi:10.1111/j.1468-2400.2006.00216.x.

   *See Schleiermacher's *The Christian FaithCh.II 'The Method of Dogmatics' pg.97-101.* This provides a clear overview of the heresies of the Christian Church to include: Pelagianism, Docetism, and Manichaeism as a few precursors to the natural heresies of the faith, to broaden the perspective and understanding of Schleiermacher.

[←11]

Lothar Schäfer, and Diogo Valadas Ponte. 2013. "Carl Gustav Jung, Quantum Physics and the Spiritual Mind: A Mystical Vision of the Twenty-First Century." *Behavioral Sciences*, no. 4: 601. doi:10.3390/bs3040601.

The Oxford handbook of religion and science / edited by Philip Clayton and Zachary Simpson, associate editor. Resourcing pg.879-882 which focuses more adamantly on the development of personhood and the interchanging relationship with the body, and mind as interpreted through the lens of the self, coming into self-awareness.

[←12]

Clendenen, Avis. 2010. "Hildegard, Jung, and the Dark Side of God." *Magistra* 16 (2): 26–76. https://search.ebscohost.com/login.aspx?direct=true&db=a9h&AN=572 76666&site=ehost-live&scope=site.

*See *The Dark Night of The Soul* by John of the Cross, Book II. Ch. IX. This read implicates the notion that through the darkness that becomes the journey into the soul, there is found the illumination of the mind and spirit which becomes inspired and elevated toward new modes of thought, and thus defends the faith through this thought.

[←13]

Chapman, G Clarke, Jr. 1997. "Jung and Christology." *Journal of Psychology & Theology* 25 (4): 414–26.
https://search.ebscohost.com/login.aspx?direct=true&db=lsdah&AN=ATLA0001019920&site=ehost-live&scope=site.

[←14]

Laurentiis, Allegra de. 2016. *Hegel and Metaphysics□: On Logic and Ontology in the System*. Hegel-Jahrbuch / Sonderband. [N.p.]: De Gruyter.
https://search.ebscohost.com/login.aspx?direct=true&db=nlebk&AN=1221910&site=ehost-live&scope=site.

[

]

Shults, F. LeRon. 2008. *Christology and Science*. Ashgate Science and Religion Series. Grand Rapids, Mich. https://search.ebscohost.com/login.aspx?direct=true&db=cat03946a&AN=APTS.142121&site=ehost-live&scope=site.

[←16]

Re Manning, Russell, and Samuel Shearn. 2018. *Returning to Tillich : Theology and Legacy in Transition*. Tillich Research = Tillich-Forschungen = Recherches Sur Tillich. Berlin: De Gruyter. https://search.ebscohost.com/login.aspx?direct=true&db=e000xna&AN=1658992&site=ehost-live&scope=site.

*See *Returning to Tillich Ch.15 Paul Tillich and The Dark Night of Faith as Mystical Experience.* This chapter carefully outlines Tillich's synthesis of "...the state of being grasped by the transcendent unity of unambiguous life–it embodies love as the state of being taken into that transcendent unity."

Printed in Great Britain
by Amazon

67664267R00045